This penetrating and shocking pictorial history of Hitler's Thousand-Year Reich is intended by its authors to be a sober reminder of a terrible past and a somber warning for future generations. The authors explain the selection of material and the purpose of their book in the following words: "From the material at our disposal we chose 240 pictures. Less would have been too little; more, too much for the human brain to grasp. And that is exactly what matters to us: that the truth be grasped; that the lesson be learned —particularly by the young who will be responsible for tomorrow."

the pictorial history

f the third reich

by **ROBERT NEUMANN** with **HELGA KOPPEL**

BANTAM BOOKS   NEW YORK   LONDON   TORONTO
A NATIONAL GENERAL COMPANY

the pictorial history of the third reich

A Bantam Book
published May 1962
2nd printing May 1962
3rd printing July 1962
4th printing January 1967
5th printing March 1967
6th printing November 1967
7th printing August 1971
8th printing January 1972
9th printing December 1973

Based on HITLER, AUFSTEIG AND
UNTERGANG DES DRITTEN REICHES
by Robert Neumann with Helga
Koppel published by Verlag
Kurt Desch, Munich.
© Copyright 1961 by
Verlag Kurt Desch

Published simultaneously in the
United States and Canada.
Bantam Books are published by
Bantam Books, Inc., a National
General company. Its trade-mark,
consisting of the words "Bantam
Books" and the portrayal of a
bantam, is registered in the
United States Patent Office and
in other countries.
Marca Registrada.
Bantam Books, Inc.
666 Fifth Avenue,
New York, N. Y. 10019
Printed in the
United States of America.

DESIGNED BY
ANTHONY LaROTONDA

CONTENTS

foreword

No effort to tell the story of Hitler's Third Reich — in words, or in pictures — can content itself with depicting only the central character. Some Germans would like us to do just that: to regard Hitler as an isolated phenomenon, an incarnation of the Devil who unhappily appeared in Germany, but who might have appeared anywhere.

Well, that is not so. And, since America's former foe is its present ally, we owe it to ourselves and to Germany as well, to see the picture whole: the Devil and the forces that made him; forces that remained after his suicide, after the downfall of the Third Reich to this very day.

The authors of this book had access to six million feet of documentary film. In addition, a vast number of previously unpublished "stills" were unearthed including photographs from private collections and from sources behind the Iron Curtain. Many of the most gruesome pictures were taken by the murderers themselves, who did not hesitate to photograph each other red-handed, with their victims, as mementos of "those great days."

From the material at our disposal we chose 240 pictures. Less would have been too little; more, too much for a single human brain to grasp. And that is exactly what matters to us: that the truth be grasped; that the lesson be learned — particularly by the young who will be responsible for tomorrow.

hitler and the third reich

He was born on April 20, 1889, at Braunau, an insignificant provincial town in the German-speaking part of the Austro-Hungarian Monarchy. Monarchs: the Hapsburgs. Religion: mostly Roman Catholic. In the capital city of Vienna: splendid old palaces, the Imperial Court, the Archbishop, the rich— and a small minority of Jews, some of them very poor refugees from Eastern Europe and its pogroms and persecutions. If you were a typical Braunau burgher, you would envy and hate far-away Vienna, hate the Hapsburgs, hate the Pope, hate the Jews, and hate the Labor Party "proletarians." But Braunau is very close to the border of the German Reich. In this district, where Czechs from nearby Bohemia were already beginning to intermingle, you would compensate for your provincial inferiority complex by identifying with the very powerful German nation across the border.

Hitler's father, born out of wedlock and named Alois Schicklgruber, was one of those Braunau burghers. He transmitted all of the local resentments, hatreds, sentiments, and dreams to Adolf. There was nothing original about them.

A combination of chance, not inconsiderable gifts as an orator and intriguer, and an enormous personal intensity enabled Hitler to carry out what others merely talked about. The one Hitler was chosen by fate from among a thousand potential Fuehrers.

Several years before Adolf was born, Alois managed to have his name changed. This small, seemingly irrelevant procedure influenced Hitler's later life. First, Schicklgruber sounds so ridiculous to German ears that a "Fuehrer" of that name would have been almost impossible. Secondly, when the facts were discovered in 1930, Hitler was a highly controversial public figure and people started guessing who his real grandfather might have been. Hitler's political enemies spread the rumor that the missing ancestor was a Jew from the town of Graz. The allegation was proved unfounded by both Nazi and anti-Nazi historians. The irony is that it was directed at a man who was by then a prophet of German racial purity and superiority. Under his own racial laws he would have been ineligible for admission to the ranks of his own bodyguard, the black-clad S.S. or indeed to any public office. It must be left to the historian or psychologist of a later age to decide how far the special virulence of Hitler's mad actions against the Jews was colored by his subconscious urge to wipe out suspicions regarding his own ancestry.

The boy was lazy at school, but produced drawings of some promise; in fact, the one of his parents' bedroom is less conventional than any of his later artistic efforts. It is not surprising, however, that his middle-class father refused to allow the boy to leave school and study art.

Hitler left Braunau after his father's death. His failures to gain admission to the Vienna Art Academy are on record. In a letter written to a friend at that time, Hitler says: "You know, without wanting to boast, I believe the world lost much by their refusal to make me a painter. Or does Fate spare me for something else?"

Whatever Hitler stated about these early years in his autobiographical book MEIN KAMPF is to be regarded with suspicion. To appeal to sentimental readers he wrote that he came from "very poor peasant stock." After his "unjustified rejection" by the Vienna art school he went on living "close to starvation level" and "worked as a casual laborer." Actually, his family, though not rich, was reasonably comfortable and did send him money. It has also been established that he never did an honest day's work as a laborer. Like so many petty-bourgeois citizens who lose their footing, he turned hobo and lived in a municipal lodging house for the jobless. He claims to have had "political discussions with the Socialists" but, according to two of his associates at that time, these were actually brawls that made him very unpopular with the other inmates and with the warden. His "reading voraciously though indiscriminately" to fill the gaps in his education amounted to, first, the texts and music of Wagnerian opera (throughout the entire course of his career Hitler was an ardent Wagnerite); secondly, a vast series of "novels" by Karl May, Hitler's favorite author, telling of the feats of a German superman among the red Indians; and thirdly, the pseudo-philosophical leaflets and broadsheets of a crank called Lanz von Liebenfels. These were scatter-brained publications with headlines such as "Are you fair-haired? Then you are a Creator and Preserver of Culture!" Included were full descriptions of the habits and vile money-lending tricks of the "Subhumans," and advice on how to define yourself—with illustrations such as, "Shape of Buttocks of Inferior Race, and Superior Race." In MEIN KAMPF, Hitler comments: "At that time, I laid and fortified the foundations of my world view; there was nothing, or very little, I added at a later age."

One of his Vienna associates describes him as "black-haired, fierce, quarrelsome, untidy, lazy, wearing a large old hat and a shabby, too-long overcoat given to him by a Hungarian Jewish old-clothes peddler." He managed to make a living by doing occasional drawings for a builder, making posters, or copying Vienna picture postcards and peddling his works in the cafés.

n 1913, aged twenty-four, he left Vienna, "disgusted with that Jew-ridden, decaying city," and went to Munich. His real disgust was later discovered to have been directed against the Austrian authorities who wanted him for military service. They eventually did catch up with him, examined him, and found him unfit. He was fit enough, however, a year later, in July 1914, when war broke out. He volunteered for military service in a Bavarian regiment, and his war record at the Western front is respectable. He was a runner between company headquarters and the trenches, and was twice wounded. He earned the Iron Cross, second class, and supposedly the Iron Cross, first class, as well. But the Regimental Records say nothing about this.

On the day of surrender in 1918, Hitler, back in Germany recovering from his second wound, was convinced that the German Army was never beaten, but stabbed in the back by Socialists and Jews at home. He also believed that the Versailles Peace Treaty was an evil and unjust conspiracy against the pure and innocent German nation by Woodrow Wilson, Lloyd George, Clemenceau, the Pope, the Freemasons, and some others—"Jews all of them" (possibly excepting the Pope); and that the Germans who signed the treaty were all traitors and criminals.

"That day," he wrote in MEIN KAMPF, "I decided to be a politician." Actually, he became an agent on the payroll of the German Army, the Reichswehr.

After the Kaiser's flight to Holland in 1918, the Weimar Republic, named for the small historic town where its founding session took place, faced an extremely difficult situation: there was the misery of a World War's aftermath, as well as demands by the Allies for very substantial reparations. The extreme Left was as hostile as the extreme Right; both could point to the vast contrast between the dismal German reality and the bright promises of Wilson's Fourteen Points.

In particular, the Reichswehr, its officers still longing for the might and splendor of the Kaiser's Monarchy, was the hotbed of anti-republican sentiments. They built up and financed a so-called Free Corps, at first to defend the eastern frontiers against Polish and Communist encroachment, then as an instrument for internal civil strife. Moreover, they hired "political instructors" and spies. Hitler joined them in Munich, a center of right wing intrigue against the embattled Berlin Republic.

itler's first assignment as a Reichswehr agent was to watch a group of local tradespeople that called itself the "German Workers' Party." He joined them; according to party history he was member number seven. With the help of oratory and intrigue, Hitler managed to be elected chairman. Then he rechristened the party The National Socialist German Workers' Party, or N.S.D.A.P.—the Nazis.

Hitler soon became important in certain upper-middle class Munich circles; so much so that another hater of the

Republic joined forces with him for a time: General Ludendorff, wartime chief of the German General Staff. Thus the stage was set for Hitler's Beer Hall Putsch of 1923.

Hitler called a mass meeting in the Court Beer Cellar. Among those attending were the Minister President of Bavaria, the General of the Munich Reichswehr garrison, and the Munich police chief. Hitler lured these three men into a side room and forced them, at gun point, to sign a document declaring that they had joined him and Ludendorff in deposing the central government of the German Republic. His new co-rulers went home and within an hour or two denounced the blackmail and withdrew their signatures. Thus, Hitler and Ludendorff were faced with the alternatives of ignominious defeat, or going it alone.

They chose the latter course, and on November 9, 1923, led their crowd through a narrow street to the wide Odeon Square. Near Marshal's Hall, a small contingent of local police stopped the marchers. When the Nazis refused to disperse there was some firing. Sixteen were killed. Ludendorff, relying on the magic powers of a general's uniform, was the only one to march on, unmolested. The moment the shots rang out, Hitler threw himself on the pavement, then rushed to a taxi and disappeared. It was an utter failure for Hitler's "revolution." Later, he covered up this defeat by making Party heroes and martyrs of the sixteen victims and by staging annual "Memorial Marches."

Hitler was caught. He, Ludendorff, and a few lesser figures were put on trial. But Bavarian judges were almost as intensely against the Republic as Bavarian revolutionaries. Ludendorff was acquitted, Hitler and some of his men were sent to "honorary confinement." After a few months of comfortable life in mock-imprisonment he was free.

In that "prison," Hitler wrote most of MEIN KAMPF. A priest named Staempfle helped him put it into publishable German. The priest revealed this fact, and, as a result, was killed when Hitler rose to power.

This marks the end of the obscure period of Hitler's life. After his release from prison, he found his party shattered but not extinct. His associates had fled abroad, or were quarreling, or had returned to their former civilian occupations. Goering, Hitler's chief lieutenant, was in a hospital in Sweden undergoing treatment for morphine addiction. (His cure was not finally effected until the Americans locked him in his cell at Nuremberg; but, though they kept the drug from him, they failed to discover the poison pill that saved him from being hanged.) Streicher, Jew-baiter number one, had been suspended for molesting little girls. Himmler, future head of the Gestapo, was a chicken farmer. Hitler's "Sturm-Abteilungen," or S.A., a private army organized by one Roehm, a homosexual, was no longer allowed to wear its uniform in many parts of Germany. But the main problem was that the man in the street had lost interest in Hitler's rallies and harangues.

After the first post-war misery, a period of prosperity revived Germany. The Allies reduced their claims for reparations; money, particularly American money, went into rebuilding German industry; production increased and the standard of living rose. At this time, the Germans had no patience with Hitler's rantings and resentments. As long as Germany was economically healthy, Hitler was sick.

But all was changed virtually overnight. In 1929, after the stock market crashed, prosperity ended everywhere. Foreign investments, on which Germany depended, were withdrawn; factories closed; unemployment and misery among workers followed and led to countless bankruptcies among small tradesmen and artisans. The workers grew more radical and swelled the ranks of the Communists; the lower middle classes, having lost much and fearing to lose the rest, also grew more radical — and here fascism had its second chance.

Hitler might not have succeeded this time either, had he not found very powerful backers. For German big business, Hitler, who had the ear of millions of impoverished citizens, was an antidote to the growing unrest among workers and workless, Socialist and Communist alike.

Hitler's dealings with big business are still the subject

of hot argument. But it has now been established that the sum given him by the industrialists was five million marks — equal in U.S. currency to a million and a quarter dollars.

The ex-hobo of Vienna could now wage murderous street brawls and election campaigns on an unprecedented scale. For that was part of Hitler's deal with industry: while he sent his toughs into the streets to fight the Communists and Socialists, he and his closest associates, were to become respectable and, hence, eligible to run for high office.

There followed the endless series of parliamentary and presidential elections that studded the final years of the Weimar Republic. Ebert had been the Republic's first president. When he died, the Germans resorted to the tradition of calling upon their pensioned-off field marshals to govern them. In Germany's case, it was Hindenburg, supreme commander in the last, lost war—honest, helpless, senile, and committed more firmly to the defunct Monarchy of the Kaiser than to the Republic he was to rule.

The parliamentary elections never led to a Hitlerite majority. But the permanent unrest forced a basically republican Chancellor, Bruening, to fall back on semi-authoritarian Emergency Laws; thus democratic traditions were first broken.

When the Nazis learned that a great deal of public money had found its way into the pockets of friends of Hindenburg's son "to help them improve their large private agricultural estates in eastern Germany," the situation was compounded. The Nazis threatened a public scandal unless Hindenburg consented to make Hitler Chancellor. Then, in November 1932, the big industrialists sent a letter to the President, urging the same course of action.

The publication of that letter caused violent controversy in Germany. The author decided to investigate the matter exhaustively. The letter was found by an American lieutenant in the ruins of a Cologne banking house. It was produced at the Nuremberg trial, but not admitted as evidence because the signatories declared it to be "merely the draft of a letter that was never sent." Indeed, the photostatic copy in my possession shows all the signatures to be in the same handwriting. However, long after the Nuremberg trials, copies of the disputed letter, signed by many of the original signatories, plus a number of new names, were discovered and are now in the Potsdam (East Germany) state archives.

Furthermore, correspondence was found between one of the signatories, Reinhart, a banker, and Meissner, Hindenburg's personal Secretary of State, from which it is clear that the whole scheme was worked out by those two men. The draft produced at Nuremberg showed the signatures of those who were invited to sign. Most of them did, some refused. There were nineteen prominent signatories in the end, financiers like Schacht and industrialists like Thyssen among them.

In any event, since no one made the conspiracy public, it is fair to say that the most influential section of German industry and banking were actively or by connivance guilty of bringing decisive pressure to bear on the senile President to make Hitler Chancellor.

Hindenburg yielded on January 31, 1933. Hitler had ridden to power on the backs of millions of panicky citizens, augmented by a rising tide of the jobless, and powerfully aided by many important men in banking and industry.

The big business men had hoped to control him. They did not, as it turned out. But he never broke their economic power. They flourished before him, they went on flourishing under him, and they—the same firms, if not always the same men—flourish in West Germany today.

A few weeks after Hitler took power, the Reichstag went up in flames. Fierce controversy still rages as to whether this highly complicated arson was done single-handedly by one van der Lubbe, a half-witted Communist youth from Holland, or by a specialist gang of Nazi incendiaries called in by Goering (from whose adjoining residence a secret subterranean corridor was discovered leading straight into the Reichstag). The head of the alleged gang, long presumed dead, is now chairman of a prosperous concern in Duesseldorf.

The Nazis used the burning of the Reichstag as a pretext

to suppress all political opposition. Even more disturbing was the fact that among the first to toe Hitler's line were the great majority of German judges, university professors, artists, actors, writers and journalists. High dignitaries of both churches, Protestant and Catholic, also tried to come to terms with Hitler, thus leaving the large, non-political masses of the German nation bewildered and in a moral vacuum. Into this void seeped the Nazi doctrine of race hatred and nihilism. The damage was already done before the best among churchmen started resisting.

In general, opposition by lone intellectuals was initially secret, powerless and unorganized; and the anti-Nazi political parties had lost their leaders through murder, arrest or flight. Also, German tradition, which called for the citizen, the "subject," to obey authority, presaged the fate of Germany.

To pass over German resistance as if nothing of that sort had ever existed would be unfair. Quite apart from Jews and foreigners, Hitler's early hanging judges passed sentence on many Germans. (Soon afterward the Fuehrer introduced beheading with an ax.— He found it more Germanic.)

After twelve years of the Thousand Year Reich, 130,000 Germans had been beheaded, hanged, or otherwise murdered by Nazis. Apart from the Army officers, intellectuals, and aristocrats who staged the attempt on Hitler's life on July 20, 1944, and apart from the Munich students' rising of the Scholl brother and sister, there has been a strange conspiracy of silence regarding most of those 130,000 victims. It was a conspiracy perpetrated by Hitler, who wanted the world to believe that an undivided nation was backing him, and abetted by his most implacable enemies — Roosevelt and Churchill — whose policy of unconditional surrender implied that virtually all Germans were Nazis. Thus the entire nation was identified with the plague.

however, those were later developments. In 1933, the vast bulk of the German nation stood squarely behind its highly successful Fuehrer and objected little to its own enslavement. By early summer of 1934, everybody and everything in Germany was under Hitler's direct control, with the exception of the Army, which had preserved a relative degree of independence, and Hitler's own vast private army of storm troopers, commanded by Roehm, who were growing restive waiting for the spoils promised by Hitler.

After much secret haggling with the Army generals and discussions with Himmler's specially trained and racially selected black-clad "élite corps," the S.S. (who hoped to be the happy heirs to the power of the S.A.), Hitler decided on a lightning purge. On June 30, 1934, Roehm, many of his underlings, and thousands of others throughout Germany were murdered.

After that day, Hitler was at the summit of his power.

What sort of a man was Hitler at that time? He was a vegetarian, a teetotaler, a non-smoker. Ever since his Vienna days, he had an irresistible craving for cream cakes and ate huge quantities of them. He took pills, vitamins, sedatives, stimulants. Injections of drugs and counter-drugs were given him by his quack personal physician. An ill-humored, lonely crank during his early years of failure, after 1933 he would force all and sundry to sit up with him until daybreak, listening to his dreary monologues.

Most of Hitler's involvements with women were neurotic. To his chalet high up in the Bavarian hills, he took his sister, Frau Raubal, as a housekeeper. Hitler fell madly in love with her young daughter, Geli. He was a jealous lover who suspected her relationship with his chauffeur. In the end, she was found shot dead in Hitler's apartment in Munich. It was said to have been a suicide. Maria Reiter was the only woman to associate with him and emerge unharmed. She had once refused him, and only years afterward, when he was famous, did she become his mistress; thereupon, he married her off to one of his storm trooper underlings.

Hitler's most enduring attachment was with Eva Braun, a young woman employed by his personal photographer, Hoffmann. Hidden away from all but his most intimate associates, she remained Hitler's mistress throughout the years of Nazi rule. He married her before their double suicide.

behind the facade of the simple life, behind "Strength through Joy" holidays and Party rallies for his guileless subjects, behind the Olympic games for gullible foreigners, Germany prepared for war. "I'd rather have it when I'm fifty than when I'm sixty," Hitler confided. He rearmed systematically, and his old friends the industrialists prospered. His famed Autobahnen, to all frontiers, were part of his preparations.

The first move, in 1936, was the march into the Rhineland, demilitarized by treaty with the Allies. We now know that the slightest counter-move by the French would have stopped this adventure.

Then, civil war broke out in Spain: the liberal-socialist republican government was assaulted by a dissident colonel, Franco, with the aid of Spanish North African regiments. The conflict might have remained localized, had not Italian dictator Mussolini decided to help his Spanish fellow-fascists by sending troops. Hitler, too, sent aircraft, technicians, and pseudo-volunteers who called themselves the "Condor Legion." In turn, the Spanish government organized an "International Brigade" from virtually all countries of the globe, and Soviet Russia sent them some aid. While the West preserved official neutrality, Hitler went all out to use Spain as a testing ground for his troops and new weapons. As a result, Franco won in the end.

Next, it was Austria's turn. In 1918, the Austro-Hungarian Monarchy had collapsed, and in German-speaking Austria, Nazi ideas had been encroaching for many years. The two main parties there were Labor, and the Catholic middle-class whose leader, Dollfuss, organized a fascist militia and smashed the workers' organizations in February 1934. He was assassinated by the Nazis a few months later. A few years later, Hitler marched into Austria and was greeted enthusiastically by a substantial part of the population.

There remains the case of Czechoslovakia. In 1938, Hitler suddenly claimed the Sudetenland for his German Reich. Alarmed, the British Conservative Prime Minister Chamberlain started a series of humiliating visits to the Fuehrer in an effort to appease him and save world peace. Finally, at Munich in the autumn of 1938, Hitler was given all he wanted — the whole of Sudetenland with all of Czechoslovakia's fortifications — on his solemn promise to leave the rest of the unhappy country alone. A few months later, Hitler seized all of Czechoslovakia.

Chamberlain and his British Conservatives, and most of the peace-loving West along with them, had yielded step by step to Hitler. Even in such matters as the Nazi persecution of the Jews, they had confined themselves to ineffectual protests. A general boycott of Jewish shops and smashing of windows in 1933 marked the beginning; then came the

Nuremberg anti-Semitic racial laws of 1935 (officially commented on by Globke, now Adenauer's Secretary of State); it culminated in the "Crystal Night" of November 1938, when the Nazis burned all Jewish synagogues in Germany and arrested and deported to unknown destinations the first 20,000 German Jews. By then even the blind could see that Hitler was ready for war. Britain and France started rearming belatedly and haphazardly, distributing gas masks, digging air raid trenches.

Last-minute political maneuvering continued during the summer and autumn of 1939. It was known that Hitler planned to turn east against Poland. But Poland was France's ally and had a British guarantee of its borders. An understanding between the West and the Soviet Union to contain Hitler's expansionism was undermined because Chamberlain mistrusted Stalin too much to consider a military pact. The Poles and Rumanians also mistrusted him and would not permit Soviet troops to enter their territories. Stalin, therefore, had an excuse for negotiating a last minute non-aggression pact with Hitler.

The purpose of the pact was to gain time, according to the official Communist line. But after Khrushchev's recent disclosures it is evident that Stalin genuinely admired the German Fuehrer. Stalin pocketed eastern Poland and the Baltic countries without qualm and he was genuinely surprised by the Nazi betrayal and attack in 1941.

In any event, the stage was set. Hitler arranged a mock-attack on a German radio station near the Polish frontier, by S.S. men and concentration camp inmates who were forced to don Polish uniforms and were then killed. And so he could announce to the world that it was mere retaliation when his troops invaded Poland on September 1, 1939. Two days later, Britain and France lived up to their treaty obligations and declared war on Hitler.

After the Polish campaign, there was a lull. In 1940, Hitler overran Denmark, Norway, Holland, Belgium, France. Hitler's effort to smash Britain by air assault failed so completely that his planned invasion by sea was never tried. Instead, in 1941, he seized the Balkans, won victories in North Africa, and, in June, staged an all-out attack on Soviet Russia — with unprecedented successes, until the Russian winter of 1942-1943 brought the turn of the tide. The British stopped Hitler at El Alamein in Egypt; the Russians stopped him at Stalingrad; the Americans landed in North Africa. In a long, slow campaign, Italy was neutralized. The summer of 1944 brought the Allied landings in Normandy. By May 1945, the Allies had freed Western Europe and occupied half of Germany, while the Red Army cleared Russia and eastern Europe.

With the exception of the first shock of the unexpected

Allied declarations of war, Hitler's vast successes through the end of 1942 gave him limitless self-confidence. Stalingrad and El Alamein made him stagger; but what really unnerved him was the attempt on his life by high-ranking officers and aristocrats.

His reactions from then on were those of a paranoid tyrant. He not only insisted that the death sentences be carried out by slow strangulation, but he ordered the deaths filmed for his private movie theater, where he viewed them again and again, uttering raucous shouts.

To the end, the Fuehrer could not come to terms with the hopeless situation. Alone among his generals, he compulsively insisted that the Germans could upset and repel the Allied encirclement. But the spine of the German Army was broken. And Hitler was a broken man whose physical deterioration was conspicuous: he trembled, his gestures were spasmodic.

When the Russians approached Berlin, he transferred his headquarters to the shelter underneath the Reich Chancellery. When the Russians were about to seize it, he staged pompous and sentimental ceremonies reminiscent of Wagner's GOET-TERDAEMMERUNG. Then he shirked final responsibility by committing suicide — with a final lie on his lips, as it were, for the Nazi radio announced that he had "died heroically on the field of battle, leading his troops."

It was the end of a nightmare.

Or was it?

By the time Germany was occupied and partitioned by the victorious Allies, the Cold War had started.

In the East, leading Nazi criminals, if they were caught, were killed—with the exception of a few useful military and civilian specialists, who are still actively working under Communist control. Young people were forgiven and permitted to swell the ranks of Communist organizations. They marched from one authoritarian system into another. But the new dictatorship is, in effect, a safeguard against the resurrection of the old. In other words, there is no danger of neo-Nazism in East Germany.

In West Germany, where most influential ex-Nazis fled because they feared the Russians, the situation is different. The bestial S.S. guards of the concentration camps consisted of 53,000 men according to Polish sources: 600 were condemned to death by the Allies, and executed; of the rest, some died, some escaped abroad, some served prison sentences. Today, most of the guilty men are free and live comfortably in West Germany. A few years ago, almost eighty percent of Foreign Office officials had served Hitler. A phenomenal number who hold high ranks in the police force served in the Gestapo. Some leading generals in the armed forces served in Hitler's Wehrmacht. And, there are hundreds in the judiciary who had been hanging judges and prosecutors in Hitler's bloody People's Courts. Other new cases come up all the time. Oberlaender, a Nazi expert on Eastern European racial policy, was retained by Adenauer as a Cabinet Minister until he reached full pension age a year ago. Despite a chorus of protests, Globke, commentator of the Nazi racial laws, was retained as Adenauer's chief administrative adviser and Secretary of State. The Ruhr corporation that built the cremation ovens, asked for a new mass cremation oven patent in the Federal Republic in 1953 — and got it.

All this should be seen in perspective. There are strong forces opposing those guilty men and denouncing them. Just how dangerous are they today? They were timeservers under Hitler and they are timeservers now. As long as West German prosperity lasts, the situation will remain under control, but what effect would an economic depression have on Adenauer's government?

This much one may say: that just as there is no neo-Nazi danger in East Germany, there is no danger of a change to Communism in the Federal Republic. That is small solace in a nation that has an unhappy knack of doing its worst.

To illustrate and explain the tragic events of Hitler's Third Reich, and to rouse your watchfulness — yours and your children's — are the ultimate aims of this book.

ROBERT NEUMANN

the rise and fall of the weimar republic

After an era of rapid industrialization and colonial expansion, the world was at peace. Never before, and never again afterward, would the middle classes be quite as satisfied with themselves and with their crowned heads of state. Queen Victoria still sat on the throne of an England basking in the glory of empire and "splendid isolation." But on the continent, the mighty German industrial machine (bottom, left), held the balance of power. Kaiser Wilhelm (below) also had fraternal and military ties with Franz Josef, ruler of the vast Austro-Hungarian Empire. And so, prosperous and secure, the German people could spend their Sundays rafting gaily down the rivers and relaxing in the parks (above).

Alois Schicklgruber poses in the resplendent uniform of a minor Imperial Hapsburg Custom Service officer. Several years after he was born to Maria Anna Schicklgruber, an unwed servant girl, she married Johann Georg Heidler, an itinerant miller. Heidler never legitimatized the boy, who continued to bear his mother's maiden name until he was past forty. At that time, long after the death of both Heidler and Maria Anna, three witnesses were found who swore before the priest that each had heard Heidler acknowledge his paternity of Alois. Accordingly the priest struck "Schicklgruber" from the parish register and replaced it with the name "Hitler." After two unsuccessful marriages, Alois, now almost fifty, married his second cousin, Klara Poelzl. The first two children born of this wedlock died in infancy. The third child, seen in his earliest known baby portrait, survived. He was named Adolf and surnamed Hitler. Although he would later make it appear that poverty and deprivation were his lot, actually, the family was quite comfortable on the father's pension. Moreover, Adolf was given the opportunity of a good education — an opportunity which his poor school record demonstrates was wasted.

Unser Adolf

"Our Adolf," seen here in a school picture, showed some promise as an artist when he was ten years old. The uncarpeted interior, with its heavy, curlicued furniture, reflects his solid, middle-class background. Later, he drafted a petty-bourgeois dream of a house; its bay windows and turrets reflect his notions of the great world. But, at the age of twenty, he was rejected by the Vienna Art Academy.

1914: the Archduke of Austria was assassinated by a Serbian nationalist, and half the world leaped headlong into war. In Munich, Hitler
joined the crowd which gathered to roar its approval. Hoffmann,
later to become Hitler's court photographer, recorded the scene.
When he learned Hitler had been there, he made an enlargement of
the old negative, and, astonishingly, found his Fuehrer in the crowd.

Two days later Hitler (right, in the center) volunteered and was accepted by the Bavarian Army. He served as a messenger, was wounded in action, rose to the rank of corporal, and was awarded the Iron Cross, second class. A fragment of poetry written in the field has survived (below); in it the enthralled nationalist sees a future dominated by a "Federation bound with somber might."

After the Revolution took Russia out of the war, the entire German army was freed for an assault on the West. In May 1918, a mighty offensive put an end to the years of indecisive trench warfare (top). But sizable units of fresh American troops helped meet the attack. The Allies then launched a fierce counterattack that pushed the Germans back along the entire front. In full retreat (center, left), the Germans capitulated even before their troops had left French soil. Little wonder that the hordes of embittered prisoners (bottom, left) thought they had been sold out. When the Allies dictated the humiliating Treaty of Versailles, Germany's rage forced Wilhelm to abdicate. Below, from left to right: Lloyd George, Orlando, Clemenceau, and Wilson representing the Big Four at the peace conference.

With defeat came economic collapse. A ruin-
ous inflation virtually wiped out the middle
class. The people pawned their last posses-
sions and queued up in front of the free soup
kitchens. The failure of the old order moved
the people to the Left. Rosa Luxemburg, seen
addressing a mass meeting, and Karl Lieb-
knecht, were the leaders. One year later, in
1919, both were murdered by Army officers.

The Reichswehr, the German Army, hated the young Republic and supported the reactionary Free Corps with their misguided adventurers and murderers. In 1923 the rightists attempted to seize power (above, right). The Putsch failed, and Kapp, its leader, fled by plane.

An early picture of the Nazi party gathered in the back room of a tavern. It is the first one in existence which shows Hitler's infamous companions. To the left: Rosenberg and Schwarz; to the right: Gregor Strasser, Himmler, Fiehler, and Streicher. Below: Hitler stands on the Marshal's Mound and addresses a thin, straggling line of veterans.

But things were not moving fast enough. In November 1923, Hitler planned a Putsch in a Munich beer celler. Of all the names on his phony proclamation, only Ludendorff had actually agreed to participate. The next morning Hitler had most of the city councillors arrested. Himmler held the barricades. The others, proceeding to Marshal's Hall, found a small detachment of police in their way. Five minutes later the "revolution" was over. To cloak this complete failure, the Nazi mythologists produced varying texts, and the artists obediently provided heroic paintings. Here we see Ulrich Graf, a Munich butcher who supposedly fell, "pulled the Fuehrer down and covered him with his body." Another version has it that "Hitler saw a girl in danger and carried her from the crowd." Actually, the Fuehrer did lead the way: he leaped into a taxi and was first off the scene.

The courts, enemies of the Republic, were not harsh with the putschists. Ludendorff, seen posing as the victor on the steps of the courthouse, was acquitted. Hitler, imprisoned in Landsberg Fortress for one year, soon began dictating MEIN KAMPF to Hess. Although the official versions later depicted suffering and privation, life in prison was pleasant and comfortable. Hitler was well-fed, had unlimited visitors, and like most of the inmates, wore gay, Tyrolean attire.

In the 1920's, well-intentioned Chancellors battled for Germany's existence. While they were successful, the Nazi movement deteriorated. Hitler — seen with Himmler, Frick, Goebbels, Err and Goering — after his release from prison, was forbidden to speak in almost all of the German provinces. At this time the S. A. uniform was also forbidden. Later, however, one province after another lifted the ban and the leaders donned their traditional brown shirts. But the movement continued to languish. Below: Hitler and Hess review a small group of middle-aged adherents.

Toward the end of 1929 the Depression struck. Germany was particularly hard hit. Misery was universal among the workers, and those small tradesmen who managed to recoup their losses were wiped out by the failure of the savings banks. Men stood in line for food; children huddled against the cold. There was no hope. Below: finally, misery carried the Red Flag and prophesied a "day of reckoning."

And so all bans were removed; again he was allowed to beat the drum.

Violence flared as the S.A. battled Communists in the streets of Berlin

spite of police efforts, demonstrations spread to all industrial cities.

There were new heroes now, such as the petty criminal Horst Wessel, killed in the street fighting; his song later became the second national anthem. Each brawl produced new "martyrs" to inspire the S.A.

The powerful interests had figured right: the drummer did his job. First he consecrated flag after flag. Later, in 1931, he allied himself with other reactionary groups. Below: The Nazis stand with their new allies. To the left are the men of the Stahlhelm, the largest German veterans' organization; at the right, in the foreground, are Goering and Roehm. In the maneuvering which followed, the Nazis consolidated most of the rightist factions.

Finally, they all wore brown uniforms and repaired to the forests where, as a single beast they raised their arms and roared SIEG HEIL!

And even the debacle of the Beer Hall Putsch was falsified into a sacrificial offering, with annual memorials that grew bigger and bigger until they were gigantic.

The men of the Ruhr are waiting for Hitler. After patiently watching and analyzing developments, they have made their choice. At a highly secret meeting in the Industry Club in Duesseldorf, Hitler and Goering completed the arrangements. Right: Hitler is seen with Schacht, the financial wizard; others in-the-know included Thyssen and Voegler.

And, overnight, the leaders acquired affluence and respectability. Before the court, Hitler swore that he was trying to gain power only through legal means. At the opera and at theater premieres, he sat with aristocratic diplomats like von Papen. Other symbols of status were his eleven room apartment and his enormous car.

In the zigzagging of the elections and parliamentary struggles, the Weimar Republic wavered and, ultimately, was undermined. Bruening and his cabinet (top, right), forced to govern by emergency decree, thereby breached the feeble structure of German democracy. But floods of Nazi election leaflets and the intrigues of von Papen and the Army did not bring victory. It led only to the weak "Cabinet of the Barons." Goering, Roehm, and Hitler were bitterly disappointed. During this time they almost despaired of seizing governmental power.

President Hindenburg, in spite of a secret letter from top industrialists who urged that Hitler be given responsibility for the government, stated that he would never name the "Bohemian Corporal" as Chancellor. Then a rumor began about government funds taken by the President's son (above). Nazi threats of a scandal finally turned the tide. "We want the Fuehrer," chanted the mob. They got what they wanted: on January 30, 1933, Hitler was given the reins of government. Ludendorff, who had fallen out with Hitler, wired Hindenburg, "I predict most solemnly that this man will die in incredible misery. Coming generations will curse you for naming him Chancellor." Right: Hitler accepts the compliments of President von Hindenburg.

hitler takes power

Four weeks later, on February 27, 1933, the Reichstag burned. Goering claimed innocence, but the world did not believe him. A list of 5,000 "suspects," previously prepared, were rounded up by the police. Chief among them was the Bulgarian Communist Dimitrov who accused his accusers in court and, incredibly, was acquitted. Goering, who had screamed for a death sentence, was given a poor half-wit called van der Lubbe (below) as his victim. On March 23, the Reichstag reconvened for a session in the Opera House. Goering watched the deputies with binoculars as Hitler asked full powers. The Communists had already been arrested or deported. The Social Democrats, sitting in the Reichstag for the last time, voted against the Nazis. All others, without exception, helped kill the Republic.

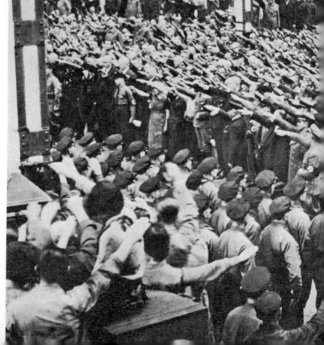

The German judges stood at attention, and due process of law was replaced by the bloody maxims of the People's Court. And the workers stood at attention as their newly appointed leader, Robert Ley, first disbanded the trade unions and stole their funds, then developed new methods of discipline — after conferring with Krupp, the head of the German munitions trust.

Whoever did not stand at attention was persecuted, banned, beaten, or taken to one of the first of the concentration camps. "I do not want any intellectuals," Hitler had said. Accordingly, on May 10, 1933, all books which displeased him were burned. Students and teachers gleefully heaped works of these writers on the flames:

Sholem Asch
Richard Beer-Hofmann
Bertolt Brecht
Max Brod
Alfred Doeblin
Lion Feuchtwanger
Leonhard Frank
Sigmund Freud
Ernst Glaeser
Ivan Goll
Jaroslav Hasek
Walter Hasenclever
Theodore Heuss
Erich Kastner
Gina Kaus
Alfred Kerr
Herman Kesten

Egon Erwin Kisch
Heinz Liepman
Heinrich Mann
Klaus Mann
Alfred Neumann
Robert Neumann
Carl von Ossietzky
Kurt Pinthus
Theodore Plievier
Erich Maria Remarque
Ludwig Renn
Arthur Schnitzler
Ernst Toller
Kurt Tucholsky
Jacob Wassermann
Arnold Zweig
Stefan Zweig

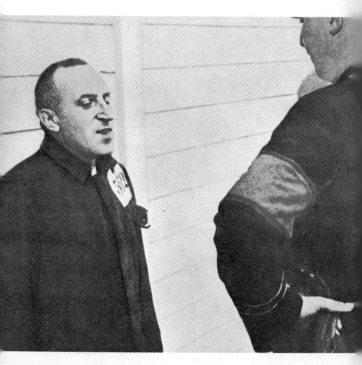

Many were imprisoned: Carl von Ossietzky
(above), winner of the Nobel Peace Prize,
was thrown into a concentration camp,
starved and subjected to physical torture.

Some went into exile or fled: the great
novelist Thomas Mann (top right), author
of THE MAGIC MOUNTAIN and BUDDEN-
BROOKS, was able to leave the country.

Others fell in line: Werner Krauss (bottom
right), now played the lead in the no-
toriously anti-Semitic movie JUD SUESS.

But the new Army is worried about Roehm, the man who walks beside Hitler at the colossal Nuremberg rallies, the man on horseback who is the acknowledged leader of the Brown Shirts, the S.A., which now numbers 4,000,000 strong.

The generals therefore invited Hitler to a confidential discussion on the battle cruiser DEUTSCHLAND (left) where an understanding was soon reached. A murderer was sent to track down Roehm. Early that morning, Hitler arrived "like a stroke of lightning" at the Munich airport. He was welcomed by Christian Weber and other high-ranking officers. Then the wholesale slaughter started. As "supreme lord of justice," Hitler declared that everything that happened was "legal." He flew to see Hindenburg and gave him his report. Then, before an adoring multitude (below), he accepted General Blomberg's thanks.

The power of the S.A. was broken; the rise of the S.S. began.

The leader of the black-shirted S.S. was Heinrich Himmler, previously a chicken farmer. As executor of the racial folly, he became the director of German frightfulness. He and his men were feared and hated throughout all Europe. Above: Hitler expresses his gratitude.

Julius Streicher, one-time elementary school teacher, suspended on charges of immorality, was one of the very few intimate friends of Hitler. Perhaps the most notorious of all the anti-Semites, his unique contribution was to merge the idiocy of racial viciousness with his own pornographic cravings. Above: Streicher displays the common touch.

In 1925, the World War I fighter pilot Goering, who fled abroad after the unsuccessful Beer Hall Putsch, was treated in Sweden as a drug addict. In 1932, he was appointed President of the Reichstag. In 1940 he would be made "Marshal of the Realm," a rank created expressly for him by his grateful Fuehrer. Without inhibition he plundered and stole works of art from those he had murdered. When the Nazis overran Europe, museums were also shamelessly looted.

Joseph Goebbels, a frustrated intellectual, had led the battles in the streets of Berlin. Wearing a trench coat, he grins and poses as victor. A superb propagandist and practitioner of the "Big Lie," he was nevertheless not quite able to sustain an image of himself as a devoted father and husband: his affairs with actresses were notorious. As press chief, he presented the official version of all important news — versions that were not to be questioned. He also ruled the theater and the radio.

The social life of Hitler's inner circle was frequently grandiose. Top, left: a gala concert at the castle of Ribbentrop, the champagne salesman with "good manners" whom Hitler appointed his Minister of Foreign Affairs. (The original owner of the castle was taken to Dachau and died there.) Bottom, left: Hitler's mistress, Eva Braun, installed as housekeeper in the Berghof, rarely appeared at public functions.

During this period a stream of foreign dignitaries paid court to Hitler. Among the visitors were the Duke and Duchess of Windsor (above).

For propaganda purposes, however, an image of the simple life was maintained — complete with "one-pot" meals and talks with elderly rustics. Thus, Hitler deliberately presented himself as being close to the people — at least while Goebbels' photographers stood by.

The youth of the country followed the Pied Piper. Hitler called the tune: "Boys and girls enter our organizations at the age of ten. Four years later, they move on to the Hitler Youth. After four more years, they are ready for the Party, the Labor Front, the S.A. and the S.S. Then to the Labor Service to be drilled for six months. . . . And never during their entire lives shall they be free."

Hitler said, "My pedagogy is hard. All weakness must be hammered away. We will bring up a youth from whom the old world will shrink in fear. I want a forcible, domineering, unflinching, cruel youth. I want to see the free splendid predatory animal spring from their eyes. Thus will I extinguish thousands of years of human domestication." And he achieved his goal. Below: The "splendid, predatory beasts" are seen after their capture at Auschwitz.

Those who played the game were decorated, advanced, and invited
to receptions at the Propaganda Ministry. And for the women who
produced many children, there was the proudly worn Mother's Cross.

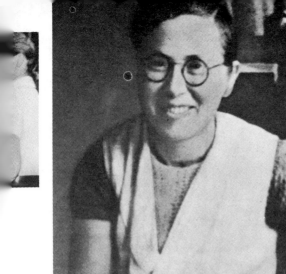

But this mother, Judith Auer, did not play the game. On the day she was executed, she wrote to her only daughter: "My beloved, small, best comrade! I have this wish: You should give your heart to something special. You want to become a kindergarten teacher. I approve this wish with all my heart. But think, at the same time, of your early experiences, my loved one, and forget sometimes what you have just now learned. Let love guide you. Mistakes made through loving are never sins. You must now bear a huge sorrow. But you must try to seek all the joy that I will no longer be able to prepare you for. . . . I must now make my last goodbyes. Remain strong and brave, my beloved. I know you will never let yourself down. I will leave gracefully and quietly. . . . Farewell and be kissed!"

111

Some German resistance persisted. 130,000 paid with their lives. But the millions fell into line. The men, like the youth and the mothers, closed ranks around their Fuehrer; and for the men acquiescence was especially easy. The uniform, the parade, and the military tradition were powerful forces. From top to bottom: marching at the turn of the century; those left over from 1870 march with the veterans of 1914; the survivors of 1914 march with the new soldiers of the Third Reich. Below: The invalids of the last war salute the madman who is now leading the world into the next one.

And the artists, too, served the master. German painters created a "German Art" to Hitler's taste. These paintings were hung in the museums, while the great works of expressionism and abstractionism were removed and shipped abroad.

Right: the Fuehrer stands at the top of his pyramid. His conquest of Germany is now complete.

the
opening
guns

In 1936 the fascist General Franco rebelled against the Spanish Republic. Hitler seized the opportunity to test new techniques of warfare. The town of Guernica (above) was coldly and systematically destroyed from the air. The bitter, bloody conflict finally came to an end in 1939. Hitler and Franco, "allies and brothers in arms," proudly paraded as joint victors. Bottom, right: most of the Germans who had fought on the side of the Republic — in the International Brigade and the German Battalion — were killed. They now lie buried in the soil of Spain.

The Italian dictator Mussolini had actually led the way. In 1922 he had seized power and founded the first fascist dictatorship. But relations between him and Hitler remained uneasy — until the Nazis gave support to Italy in her war against Ethiopia. This was the beginning of the Berlin-Rome Axis. The infamous alliance was celebrated with military pomp in each of the respective capitals: in Rome (left), Hitler stood beside Mussolini and Victor Emmanuel III; then, in Berlin (right), the Duce stood beside the Fuehrer on the reviewing stand. In later years (bottom), Mussolini would try to restrain his increasingly powerful comrade-in-arms from warlike adventures — a pattern that started in 1938 during the crisis over Austrian Anschluss.

Chancellor Dollfuss (top, left), though opposed to Hitler, had established his own brand of clerical fascism in Austria. But, by smashing the unions and undermining democratic processes he had actually helped to clear the way for the Germans. On July 25, 1934, he was assassinated by Austrian members of the Nazi Party. As an alibi, Hitler had arranged to attend a performance of Wagner's RHEINGOLD; but his adjutants kept coming into his box to whisper news of the developments to him. Friedelind Wagner recalls, "It was terrible to watch. . . . He could scarcely wipe the delight from his face." Schuschnigg (bottom, left), seen listening to German Foreign Minister Neurath, succeeded Dollfuss after the Nazi Putsch failed. But he could not stay the course of fate. When Hitler marched into Vienna in 1938, the Austrian police force received him with the Nazi salute.

The people of Vienna also received their new Fuehrer with the traditional salute. Hitler told the wildly enthusiastic crowd that he would transform Austria unto "a flower garden." But, starting on the very day of this seemingly joyous Anschluss, the arrests began. 63,000 suspects were secretly taken to the concentration camps and political prisons that had already been established by the Austrian fascists. An occasional public hanging was provided as a warning to the resistance; but most of the murders occurred in secret (right).

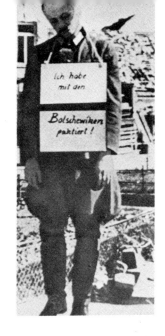

Later in 1938, Hitler made his "last territorial demand"—the Sudetenland. British Prime Minister Chamberlain flew to Berchtesgaden and Godesberg, determined to avoid war at any cost. Then, in Munich, he was joined by French Premier Daladier and Mussolini.

A map of Czechoslovakia was put on the table, new borders were drawn; the fate of the Czechs was settled without consulting them. Below: Chamberlain returned to England happily claiming "peace in our time." But the glum Daladier saw the situation more realistically.

In May 1939, Hitler provoked a second Czechoslovakian crisis. Without allies, their border defenses, railroads, and heavy industry crippled by the Munich sell-out, the Czechs yielded. The aged President Hacha, after suffering a heart attack during the negotiations with Hitler, agreed not to resist the German advance. When the Nazis marched in, reviewed by their Fuehrer, they found the streets completely deserted. But in Prague, young Czechs massed to meet the German soldiers with desperation and fury. This was to be the last of Hitler's "bloodless" coups. The occupation of the Rhineland, the Anschluss, the annexation of the Sudetenland, and the rape of Czechoslovakia had followed in bewildering succession. Hitler had gained enormously in war-making potential and in prestige. But, at long last, the disastrous era of appeasement was drawing to a close.

Inside Germany the pace had quickened. In 1933, storm troopers had stood in front of stores and shouted anti-Semitic obscenities. In 1938, a crowd of ordinary Viennese citizens and school boys force a child to inscribe the word "Jew" on the door of his own house.

One man, Walter Poetsch (above), dared speak against the nation-wide madness: "Human beings, because they are of Jewish origin, are mocked, boycotted, maltreated and killed. Hundreds of German Jews have been killed since 1933. Thousands have been beaten, cruelly tortured, thrown into concentration camps: physicians who once self-sacrificingly helped us, scientists, artists, lawyers, business-men, workers. Tens of thousands were thrown out of their jobs, exposed to dire poverty without any means of support. Hundreds of thousands are made outcasts by arbitrary force and more arbitrary laws: fellow creatures, human beings like ourselves." Poetsch vanished; nothing is known of his fate. And then, in November 1938, with the "Crystal Night," the horror entered its most terrible phase. Above: in that single night all German synagogues were de-secrated or destroyed. 20,000 people were rounded up and taken away. Left: how many of those who look on and laugh are still among us, living in comfort and claiming they knew nothing of these atrocities?

The national madness was kept at fever pitch with thanksgiving celebrations, athletic festivals, mass-marriages — and the keynote was "Strength through Joy!" Uniforms became more and more prominent, and the massive parades of military might gave life a vital new focus and meaning.

By 1939 it was clear that war was inevitable. The only question was whether Hitler would strike against the East or the West. But the Allies distrusted the Russians too much to consider a treaty with them. In the last-minute maneuvering, Stalin signed a pact with the Germans (above). Back in Berlin, Ribbentrop received his Fuehrer's thanks (right). Now Hitler's war could begin.

the holocaust

Hitler had given his generals their secret orders. "The propaganda occasion I shall supply," he had stated. On August 31, 1939, tanks and planes were ready, hidden by trees along a road on the German side of the frontier. Then reports of a Polish attack on a German radio station began pouring in. Hitler stood before the Reichstag

"Since 5:45 this morning, we have begun shooting back," he said.

The planes flew to their appointed destinations. Below: Warsaw, 1939.

Then the tanks and motorized infantry crashed through the Polish lines. This was the new kind of warfare that Hitler's generals had perfected in Spain. No match for the superior armor, their communications shattered by the lightning advance, the Poles (below) retreated or were captured and herded into prison camps by victorious Germans.

Nazi blitzkrieg and Russian invasion destroyed the partially mobilized Polish army in barely more than a month. Even before the campaign was over, Field Marshals Manstein and Reichenau had issued orders of the day telling their soldiers that they were more than dedicated warriors, they were also "carriers of an implacable national ideal . . . and, hence, pledged to extermination of racial inferiors once and for all." The persecutions began in the towns and villages. Even the oldest women were examined with a whip to see if they were useful as workers. But simple brutality was not enough when the goal was genocide.

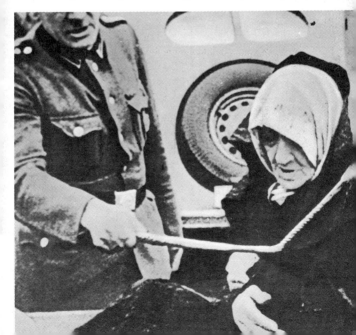

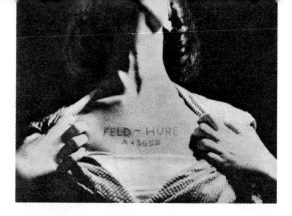

Girls were forced into military brothels and inscriptions were burned over their breasts. Stars of David were branded on the heads of men. And beards of old Jews were set afire for the amusement of the soldiers who stood by and laughed.

But racial madness called for more systematic methods. Throughout occupied Europe thousands were seized, herded into freight cars, and never let out until the trains reached the sidings at Buchenwald, Dachau, and the dozen other new S. S. concentration camps. Those who were suitable "to be worked to death" were separated, given uniforms, and tattooed. The others would be used for experiments on the effects of intense cold, extremes of pressure, poisons, and certain surgical operations. For the slave laborers, there were daily floggings, watery soup, beds of straw, inadequate clothing, and constant surveillance by guards who dragged off anyone who faltered.

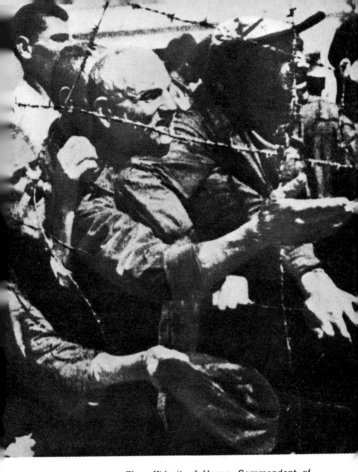

The affidavit of Hoess, Commandant of Auschwitz until December 1, 1943, states that at least 500,000 of the slave laborers died of exhaustion in this camp alone.

Incredibly, most of the prisoners clung to life. But when life was too much to bear, there was a quick way out: suicide on the electric fence.

In the meanwhile, all was quiet on the Western Front. This was the period of the "Phony War." During the winter of 1939 and the early spring of 1940, peace feelers were put out. A fierce battle was conducted with leaflet bombardments and radio barrages, while the French poilus played cards and the British tommies sang of "Hanging out their washing on the Maginot Line." Right: a section of the French defenses. The Nazis used the lull to mount an attack in the North.

On April 9, 1940, Germany marched into
Denmark and occupied the entire country
before noon. That same day their troops
landed at six strategic Norwegian ports.
Supported by a small British and French
expeditionary force, the Norwegians fought
back bravely. Heavy losses were inflicted
on German naval units (left), but the
Nazis managed to land 100,000 troops
(above) — more than twice the strength of
the defenders. Though they held on at
Narvik until June, the bulk of the Allied
forces had been withdrawn by the middle
of May. King Haakon and his government
fled to London, but Vidkun Quisling, whose
name has now become a synonym for trai-
tor, set up a puppet regime under Hitler.

The blitzkrieg struck next in the West. On May 10, 1940, Hitler invaded the Netherlands, Belgium, and Luxemburg. By now the pattern was familiar: armored panzer divisions swept in under an invincible cover of air power; in spite of French and British aid, the Dutch surrendered in four days, and the Belgians in less than three weeks. By this time the Germans had outflanked the Maginot Line, which they then proceeded to pierce, and took Verdun.

he British troops were driven toward the sea. Almost encircled, they ought off the Nazis night and day while a vast armada of ships evacuated 335,000 men who lined up and waded out as their turns came.

After Dunkirk the panzers rolled across France. Ten days later the Nazis marched into Paris. Churchill, who had succeeded Chamberlain, appealed for an Anglo-French Union to continue the battle; but the French Government, now in Vichy and under Marshal Pétain, sued for peace. Below: taunted by a German, a stunned poilu faces defeat.

Hitler now attempted to bomb the British into submission. Huge formations of planes struck at London and nearby cities. Coventry (top, right) was devastated. But the British slept in the subways, shot down hundreds of Nazi aircraft, and cleaned up between raids. Finally, Hitler gave up.

Britain's life-lines stretched thousands of miles across the Atlantic and through the Mediterranean Sea. Convoys provided the best defense against the U-boats and the surface raiders. Above: survivors being rescued. Below: the blazing death of a Nazi pocket-battleship.

One week before Pétain had sued for peace, Mussolini's troops had stabbed into France. Four months later they paraded into Greece, but by December, had fallen back into Albania. In March 1941, Hitler moved to support his faltering partner by striking at Greece and Yugoslavia. Balkan resistance ceased in April, Crete fell the following month. By June, 150 divisions were poised for the assault on Russia. The blitzkrieg, seen on this page, quickly swept across 550 miles.

Then the icy blasts swept down from the Arctic. Expecting a six-week war, the Germans had not issued winter uniforms. Now, stopped at the very gates of Moscow by the incredible cold, the stunned Nazis were sent reeling back by a counteroffensive along a front that reached from Leningrad to the Sea of Azov. With temperatures below zero, the Russians recaptured Rostov — the first major Nazi defeat.

The horror was no longer confined to concentration camps. After the invasion of Russia, Hitler and Himmler organized S.S. extermination squads—the Einsatzgruppen. Hundreds of thousands were slaughtered in the field. First the victims were forced to dig mass trenches; then whole families were shot and toppled into the shallow graves. Later, mobile gas vans were used. Did anyone protest? One German officer (shot in Dachau, 1945) reported: "... 30,000 Jews were butchered in little more than an hour. And since the machine guns ran out of ammunition, flame throwers were used. And the men who were off duty all crowded around to see the spectacle: young lads of nineteen and twenty.— Oh the shame! Oh life without honor!"

en were dragged behind cars and then left to bleed and scream until
ad. Others were actually beaten to death with iron pipes. Field
arshal Kesselring favored even more public displays: his orders were
hang men under bridges and trestles and allow them to swing as
arnings to a hostile populace. But as the brutality increased, and
e warnings became more fanatical, the resistance grew stronger.

en Heydrich the hangman was killed by Czechs, every man, woman,
d child in Lidice was killed; then the village was burned to the ground.

But the Resistance fought on. Partisan bands were organized throughout occupied Europe. Punishment and reprisals were swift and deadly
but sabotage increased and guerilla attacks became more daring
Top, right: the last of the last. After millions of Jews had been killed
under the most appalling conditions, the last survivors of the Warsaw
Ghetto would not consent to yield without bitter, heroic resistance
Bottom: memorial tablets erected by the French for German partisans

LISA OST
PARTISANE ALLEMANDE
MORTE POUR LA LIBERTÉ
ASSASSINÉE
PAR LA GESTAPO
TROUVÉE DANS LE PUITS
DE CÉLAS

HEDWIG ROBENS
PARTISANE ALLEMANDE
MORTE POUR LA LIBERTÉ
ASSASSINÉE
PAR LA GESTAPO
TROUVÉE DANS LE PUITS
DE CELAS

In December, 1941, while the Russians were counterattacking and the British were driving back to El Agheila, the Japanese made their infamous attack on Pearl Harbor. Then, in 1942, while the Japanese triumphed in the Philippines and the Indies, Rommel (above) swept to within seventy miles of Alexandria. But the British held at El Alamein and counterattacked in October (bottom, right). Meanwhile, convoys were landing the Allies in Morocco and Algeria (top, right). By spring, the vaunted Afrika Korps had ceased to exist.

The American Seventh Army, under General Patton, and the British Eighth, under General Montgomery, next moved against Sicily. 3,000 ships and transport planes carrying paratroopers, landed an invasion force of 160,000 on the island. Germans and Italians fought bitterly at first, but, on July 23, Palermo was surrendered without a shot. With the capture of Messina in mid-August, the campaign was over.

Three weeks before the fall of Messina, Mussolini was deposed by the Fascist Grand Council and replaced by Marshal Badoglio. The Italians then surrendered to the Allies. But the Nazis seized Rome (above) and northern Italy. More than a year of bitter, bloody fighting remained ahead. Below: an Italian girl greets advancing Allied troops.

But the terrible crimes continued without abatement. Above: this prisoner is going to die. Accompanied by music, he is being pulled to the gallows. The song prescribed was "All the Birds Are Here."

Though the horror of the concentration camps remains beyond comprehension, the Nazia mania was yet to produce its most fiendish device: the extermination camp. The Gerstein document supplies evidence: . . . then Pfannenstiel (Dr. Pfannenstiel, Head of the Department of Hygiene at the University of Marburg, S.S. Major, and now physician at a fashionable spa) said, "Well, and what did the Fuehrer want?" Globocnik: " 'Faster,' he said, 'The whole business has to be done faster!' " Himmler and Eichmann, and the chemists and engineers then devised the infernal machine that Hitler had requested.

After arriving at Auschwitz or Mauthausen, those who were not capable of slave labor were immediately sent to the gas chambers. The condemned were told they were being taken to the showers and were instructed to undress. They were then herded into the large, bare rooms and locked inside. Rudolf Hoess describes the operation: "The 'final solution' of the Jewish problem meant the complete extermination of all Jews in Europe. I was ordered to establish extermination facilities at Auschwitz. At that time there were three other extermination camps: Belzek, Treblinka, and Wolzek. I visited Treblinka to find out how they carried out their extermination. The Camp Commandant told me that he had liquidated 80,000 in the course of one half year. He was principally concerned with liquidating all the Jews from the Warsaw ghetto. He used monoxide gas and I did not think his methods were very efficient. So at Auschwitz I used Cyclon B, which was a crystallized prussic acid dropped into the death chamber. It took from three to fifteen minutes to kill the people in the chamber, according to climatic conditions. We knew when the people were dead because their screaming stopped. We waited about half an hour before we opened the doors. After all the bodies were removed, our special commandos took off the rings and extracted gold from the corpses' teeth. Two and a half million were executed at Auschwitz."

Above: "Foundation Hackenholt," a primitive gas chamber. The newly
arrived prisoners were herded into the room until there was no room
for anyone to fall. The room was then filled with exhaust fumes from
a diesel engine. It took up to half an hour before everyone had died.
Right: Ilse Koch, wife of the commander of Buchenwald had prisoners
with "interesting" tattoo marks killed so that their skin could be
used for lampshades. The barbarism of the S.S. also included shrink-
ing heads, although an order forbade these and "similar gifts."

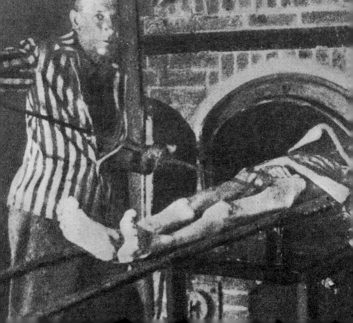

With the aid of engineers from Germany's leading industrial concerns, huge cremateria, which could handle 2,000 corpses at one time, were developed. An extermination camp prisoner describes the ovens in operation: "The flames leaped up from the new crematorium behind our barracks. At first there was a thin wisp of smoke. Then heavy gray clouds covered the sky over the camp. The wind blew these clouds in our direction. They smelled of burning flesh. Somehow it was as if a goose was burning in an oven, only much stronger. I could hardly breathe. Suddenly there was a screaming of thousands of voices. 'That's coming from the pit,' said Irene. 'They are burning them alive!'" Top: Himmler inspecting Mauthausen.

Of the 53,000 S.S. men who managed the concentration and extermination camps, a total of 600 have been brought to justice.

D-Day, June 6, 1944: In the greatest military operation of all time, 5,000 ships covered by an umbrella of 11,000 planes poured British, American, and Canadian troops onto the Normandy beaches. Although successful paratroop and glider drops had been made several hours earlier, the men waded ashore into fierce Nazi gun fire. After sufficient strength was gathered, the Nazi positions were charged and taken. Before the end of the month, Cherbourg was captured and soon a slashing offensive cut into Belgium. Bottom, right: partisans helped in the Allied advance.

Paris was liberated on August 23, 1944. 50,000 Frenchmen battled the Nazis for six days before the Allies marched in. Brussels was liberated on September 3, and Aachen, in Germany, fell late in October. But before the Allies were able to pierce the Siegfried Line, the Nazis launched a last, furious counteroffensive which sent their armor crashing fifty miles into Belgium. By Christmas the "bulge" was contained. Right: Nazi resistance crumbled before the renewed attack.

The turning point in the war against Russia had been at Stalingrad. After a massive, five-month battle, the German Sixth Army surrendered to the Reds in January 1943. That same month the siege of Leningrad was lifted. From that moment on the Russians took the initiative and drove the Nazis back all along the 1300-mile front. A new offensive was launched in June 1944, to coincide with the Allied landings in Normandy. This attack swept the Soviet armies into East Prussia by November. Above: the way back; right: German prisoners.

Hitler: "When a people are led toward perdition by a governmental power, then every member of the community has not only a right but a duty to rebel. The right of men stands above the right of the state!" When Colonel Stauffenberg and a group of officers realized that the war was lost, they tried to save what still remained. Below: Hitler, Himmler, and behind them Mussolini and Goering on their way to the site of the attempt on Hitler's life. Right: the men of July 20, 1944, face the court after their poorly organized bomb plot failed. All of them were strangled with piano wire — on special orders from Hitler. Thousands were tried in secret, other thousands killed without trial.

The Red Army rolled on. From his underground bunker Hitler ordered an all-out attack on the troops besieging Berlin. Women and children were recruited, but the offensive never developed. In their air raid shelters, the people listened to hysterical propaganda broadcasts which still promised victory; when the all-clear sounded, they stepped out into a devastated world, searched hurriedly for food and water, then rushed back to the shelters when the next alarm sounded (below).

The city lay in ruins. Children manned the defenses (left) as the Russians entered. Below: Russian tanks rumbled through the streets; and the prisoners now wore German uniforms. On the night of April 26, the Russians, began to shell the Chancellery and Hitler's bunker.

General Weidling was sent out of the bunker with orders to carry on the battle to the last member of the Hitler youth. Goebbels, whose incinerated corpse was photographed by the Russians, took poison. Hitler, seen here in his last picture, shot himself. Then, in the Chancellery garden (above), his body was soaked with gasoline and burned.

On May 7, 1945, the unconditional surrender of Germany was signed. This was the end of the Thousand Years of Hitler's Third Reich

"If you seek his monument, look around."

epilogue

It was over: the most terrible night-mare that mankind had endured. The total number of Nazi murders —not including bomb and battle dead—has been estimated, but the figures are beyond human compre-hension: 7,000,000 Russian civil-ians and almost 3,000,000 prison-ers of war; 6,000,000 Jews; more than 5,000,000 Poles; and the hun-dreds of thousands in all of the occupied countries. The cost in hu-man suffering cannot be measured.

Miraculously, a few of the tormented did survive. They emerged, Laz-arus-like, from the mouth of the tomb itself. Mankind can never expiate the sum of their misery. But have the murderers and the torturers been judged and punished so that they can never strike again?

What kind of world has been rebuilt from the ruins? Have the last days of the old and broken who survived been made bearable? Above all else, what has been done for the children—the orphaned, the sick, the crippled, the homeless? Their lost innocence can never be re-deemed. But were they given peace to overcome despair and to rebuild their will-to-live? Was there a mira-cle more wondrous than the surviv-al of their bodies: have they found the love that alone can triumph over hatred and restore their souls?

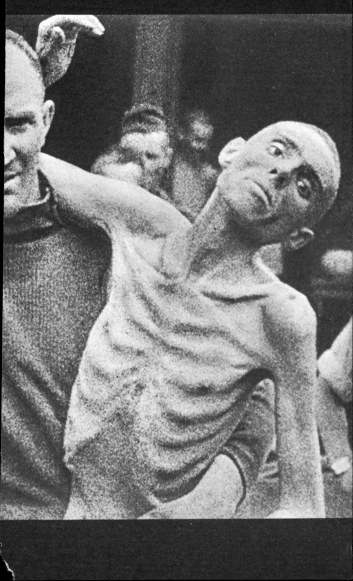

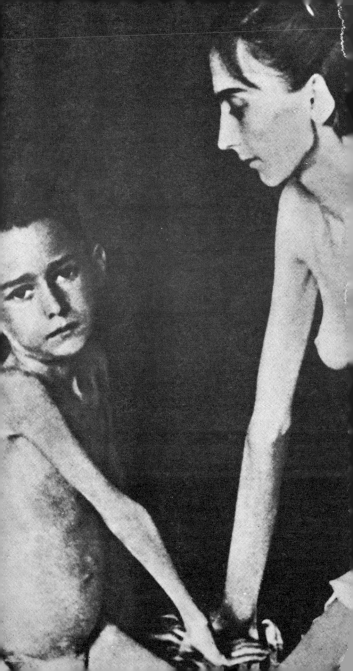

Polish?
German?
Jewish?
Christian?

Whose child?

Your child?

Alone, in a bombed-out world.

. . . England?
Russia?
Italy?

. . . Yesterday?
Today?
Tomorrow?

PHOTOGRAPHS FROM
HITLER—AUFSTIEG UND UNTERGANG DES DRITTEN REICHES:

ADDITIONAL PHOTOGRAPHS ESPECIALLY SELECTED FOR
THE PICTORIAL HISTORY OF THE THIRD REICH:

that she was able to smile at the girl and forgive her for having stolen again what she had restored.

It was the break-up of the Pollard gang, the sudden disaffection of their newest and most brilliant member. Joe himself was financed by Elizabeth Cornish and opened a small string of small-town hotels.

"Which is just another angle of the road business," he often said, "except that the law works with you and not agin you."

But he never quite recovered from the restoration of the Lewison money on which Elizabeth and Terry both insisted. Neither did Denver Pete. He left them in disgust and was never heard of again in those parts. And he always thereafter referred to Terry as "a promising kid gone to waste."

MAX BRAND

THE MASTER OF TWO-FISTED WESTERN ADVENTURE

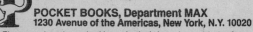